A dump truck can carry huge amounts of building material.

Earth drills are used to drill very deep holes in the ground.

A crane lifts and moves very heavy items around a building site.

The tires on a dump truck have a deep tread, and so they grip the ground well.

Whoosh!

The body of a dump truck is tipped up on big hinges to empty out the rubble or dirt.

The engine is very powerful so it can drive easily over rough tracks and mud.

Some dump trucks are so big they cannot fit on roads!

Backhoe loader

The proper name for a digger is a backhoe loader. The backhoe loader is one of the most important vehicles found on a construction site.

The teeth on a backhoe bucket help it dig deep into the ground.

The seat inside the cab can turn all the way around, allowing the driver to face the shovel at the front or the bucket at the back.

The shovel scoops up heavy loads of soil and rubble.

These mighty machines are usually brightly painted for safety - colors like yellow and orange are easy to see.

Crunch!

The backhoe bucket can be swapped for other attachments, such as grapples, hammers, and drills.

Backhoe loaders can also do stunts. "Digger dancing" can be seen at country fairs around the world!

Cement mixer truck

A cement mixer truck combines sand or gravel with water and cement to make concrete, mixing it all together in its large drum.

A "chute man" tells the driver when to send cement out of the drum and down the chute.

Vroom!

The chute can move in different directions to pour the cement where it is needed.

Inside the drum is a spiral blade that keeps the cement moving so it doesn't set.

The drum turns to mix the concrete as it travels, so that it's ready to use when it gets to the construction site.

Whoosh!

Trucks that help us

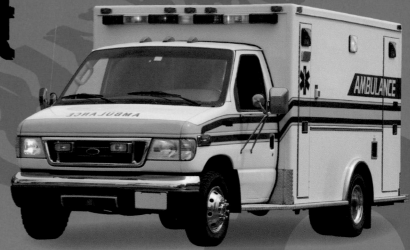

Ambulances are used to transport sick or injured people to hospital.

A flatbed tow truck is a vehicle used to transport cars that have broken down.

A rescue 4x4 can help in emergency situations that are difficult for other road vehicles to get to.

Fire engines carry firefighters and equipment to the scene of an emergency.

A garbage truck can also be called a sanitation truck or a trash truck.

Salt trucks are also called salt spreaders because they spread salt across roads to keep them free of ice.

SPREADING

Fire engine

A fire engine is an emergency vehicle that allows firefighters to get to the scene of a fire quickly.

wee-Woo!

Sirens and flashing lights warn other motorists that a fire engine is approaching.

Vroom!

FIRE DEPT.

Some fire engines have ladders to help firefighters get closer to fires in tall buildings.

Many fire engines have a huge onboard water tank. They can also suck water in from a hydrant or lake.

A large hose is connected to the fire engine's pump and water supply.

Lots of different equipment is kept in lockers on the side of the vehicle.

Garbage truck

A garbage truck is a large vehicle that carries trash from houses and businesses to a sorting center.

A garbage truck collects trash and contains it in a part of the vehicle known as the hopper.

Clank!

The dumpster hooks onto arms at the back of the truck and is lifted up.

Crunch!

DANGER
Keep clear of moving parts

A garbage truck can weigh as much as five elephants!

Garbage trucks take waste that cannot be recycled to landfill sites.

At the front of the truck is the cab.

A lot of our garbage can be recycled. Recycled garbage is made into new things for us to use.

Other mighty machines

Hooklift trucks remove dumpsters full of construction and demolition waste from building sites.

Road trains travel long distances, pulling two or more trailers at once.

A tractor-trailer, also known as a semitruck, is made up of a driving cab and a long trailer.

Monster trucks have extremely large wheels and are used mainly in competitions.

Tanker trucks transport liquids and gases from place to place.

Car transporters are used to carry and transport other vehicles.

A military tank is a strong, armored vehicle equipped with guns and caterpillar tracks instead of wheels.

Tractor

Tractors are used mostly on farms, where they pull equipment such as trailers, ploughs, cultivators, and mowers.

Early tractors were steam-powered. Nowadays they are usually powered by diesel.

A tractor's engine needs to be very powerful to help it lift and pull heavy loads.

Most tractors are restricted to a top speed of 20 miles per hour.

Chug!

Thick, chunky tires on a tractor help it to travel across very muddy ground without getting stuck.

Tanker truck

Tanker trucks are used to transport liquids such as concrete, milk, water, gasoline, diesel, and industrial chemicals. Some tanker trucks also transport gases.

The tank of a tanker truck can usually carry up to 9,000 gallons.

The tank can have up to four compartments to hold different types of liquids.

Tanker truck cargo can often be dangerous. The liquids can be flammable, corrosive, poisonous, or even explosive.

Landing legs help support the trailer when loading and unloading.

Tanker trucks are also used to fuel aircraft at airports.

The largest tanker trucks can have as many as 18 wheels.

Monster trucks

Monster trucks have become a common sight at car shows and tractor pulling competitions. The most well-known of all monster trucks is called Bigfoot.

Competitions are held all over the world, but the world finals are held in Las Vegas every March.

The tires on a monster truck are huge - about the size of a grown man!

The driver of a monster truck has to wear a safety harness, helmet, gloves, a fire suit, and a neck support.

In competitions, monster trucks perform wheelies, jumps, donuts, and freestyle.